Ramadan Journal

Let's Make the Most of this Blessed Month

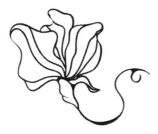

This Journal Belongs To :

_____

_____

Year :

_____

"O you who have believed,
decreed upon you is

fasting

as it was decreed
upon those before you
that you may become

righteous."

[Al Qur'an 2 : 183]

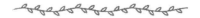

Ramadan Journal

BISMILLAAHIR-RAHMAANIR-RAHIIM

In the Name of Allah, Most Gracious, Most Merciful.

All praise and thanks are due to Allah, and peace and blessings be upon His Messenger.

CONTENT :

"This is a month,
the **FIRST** of which brings
ALLAH's mercy,
the **MIDDLE** of which brings
His forgiveness and the
LAST of which brings
emancipation from the
fire of Jahannam."

[Sahih Bukhari]

Ramadan at a glance

O Allah, help me remember You, to be grateful to You,
and to worship You in an excellent manner.

1	2	3	4	5
6	7	8	9	10
11	12	13	14	15
16	17	18	19	20
21	22	23	24	25
26	27	28	29	30

"Whoever **prayed at night** the whole month of **Ramadhan** out of **sincere faith** and hoping for a reward from **ALLAH,** then all his previous **sins will be forgiven.**"

Imam Bukhari

My Ramadan Goals

CONNECTION TO ALLAH

GOAL:	HOW TO MAKE IT HAPPEN:	✓

GOAL:	HOW TO MAKE IT HAPPEN:	✓

GOAL:	HOW TO MAKE IT HAPPEN:	✓

My Ramadan Goals

GOOD HABITS TO CULTIVATE

GOAL:	HOW TO MAKE IT HAPPEN:	✓

GOAL:	HOW TO MAKE IT HAPPEN:	✓

GOAL:	HOW TO MAKE IT HAPPEN:	✓

My Ramadan Goals

BAD HABITS TO REMOVE

GOAL:	HOW TO MAKE IT HAPPEN:	✓

GOAL:	HOW TO MAKE IT HAPPEN:	✓

GOAL:	HOW TO MAKE IT HAPPEN:	✓

"Ramadhan
is the (month) in which
was sent down

the Qur'an,
as a guide to mankind,
also clear (signs) for

guidance to
mankind
and

judgement
(between right and wrong)."

[Al Qur'an 2 : 185]

Qur'an Recitation Checklist

"You Alone we worship; You Alone we ask for help."
[Al Qur'an 1 : 5]

JUZ'		DATE:	✓
1	Al Fatiha 1 – Al Baqarah 141		
2	Al Baqarah 142 – Al Baqarah 252		
3	Al Baqarah 253 – Al Imran 92		
4	Al Imran 93 – An Nisaa 23		
5	An Nisaa 24 – An Nisaa 147		
6	An Nisaa 148 – Al Ma'idah 81		
7	Al Ma'idah 82 – Al An'am 110		
8	Al An'am 111 – Al A'raf 87		
9	Al A'raf 88 – Al Anfal 40		
10	Al Anfal 41 – At Taubah 92		
11	At Taubah 93 – Hud 5		
12	Hud 6 – Yusuf 52		
13	Yusuf 53 – Ibrahim 52		
14	Al Hijr 1 – An Nahl 128		
15	Bani Isra'il 1 – Al Kahf 74		

NOTES:

"And your **Lord** says,
Call upon Me;
I will **respond** to **you**."

[Al Qur'an 40 : 60]

Qur'an Recitation Checklist

JUZ'		DATE:	✓
16	Al Kahf 75 – Ta Ha 135		
17	Al Anbiyaa 1 – Al Hajj 78		
18	Al Muminun 1 – Al Furqan 20		
19	Al Furqan 21 – An Naml 55		
20	An Naml 56 – Al Ankabut 45		
21	Al Ankabut 46 – Al Ahzab 30		
22	Al Ahzab 31 – Yaseen 27		
23	Yaseen 28 – Az Zumar 31		
24	Az Zumar 32 – Fussilat 46		
25	Fussilat 47 – Al Jathiya 37		
26	Al Ahqaf 1 – Az Zariyat 30		
27	Az Zariyat 31 – Al Hadid 29		
28	Al Mujadila 1 – At Tahrim 12		
29	Al Mulk 1 – Al Mursalat 50		
30	An Nabaa 1 – An Nas 6		

"Our Lord, accept [this] from us. Indeed You are the Hearing, the Knowing."

[Al Qur'an 2 : 127]

NOTES:

"In every day and every night, during the month of Ramadan, there are people to whom Allah grants freedom from the Fire, and there is for every Muslim a supplication which he can make and will be granted."

[Imam Ahmad and Ibn Majah]

Du'a List

Bismillaahir-Rahmaanir-Rahiim

PERSONAL
What do I need most? Think of both Deen and Dunya.

✓

Du'a List

Bismillaahir-Rahmaanir-Rahiim

FAMILY
What do my family members need most?

_____ ✓

_____ ☐

_____ ☐

_____ ☐

_____ ☐

_____ ☐

_____ ☐

_____ ☐

_____ ☐

_____ ☐

_____ ☐

Du'a List

Bismillaahir-Rahmaanir-Rahiim

FRIENDS & THE UMMAH AT LARGE
How can I help them?

✓

The Messenger of ALLAH (S.A.W) said ...

"Whoever **feeds** a fasting person will have a **reward** like that of the fasting person, without any reduction in his regard."

[At-Tirmidhi]

Sadaqah List

Bismillaahir-Rahmaanir-Rahiim

PERSON / ORGANIZATION	IN KIND	✓

"As for he who GIVES
and who is
mindful of ALLAH,
And believes in
the best [reward],
We shall smooth his way
towards EASE."

[Al Qur'an 92 : 5-7]

Sadaqah List

Bismillaahir-Rahmaanir-Rahiim

PERSON / ORGANIZATION	AMOUNT	✓

Notes

Weekly
Suhoor & Iftar
Planner

"Have Suhoor for verily there is blessing in it."

[Abu Dawud]

Weekly Meal Planner

1 – 7 RAMADAN

	SUHOOR	IFTAR
1 RAMADAN		
2		
3		
4		
5		
6		
7		

Grocery List

BUDGET:

PRODUCE

- ☐
- ☐
- ☐
- ☐
- ☐
- ☐

MEAT / POULTRY / FISH

- ☐
- ☐
- ☐
- ☐
- ☐
- ☐

DAIRY / EGGS

- ☐
- ☐
- ☐
- ☐

GRAINS / BREAD / PASTA

- ☐
- ☐
- ☐
- ☐
- ☐

BEVERAGES / SNACKS

- ☐
- ☐
- ☐
- ☐

NON-FOOD ITEMS

- ☐
- ☐
- ☐

Weekly Meal Planner

8 – 14 RAMADAN

	SUHOOR	IFTAR
8 RAMADAN		
9		
10		
11		
12		
13		
14		

Grocery List

BUDGET:

PRODUCE

- [ ]
- [ ]
- [ ]
- [ ]
- [ ]
- [ ]

MEAT / POULTRY / FISH

- [ ]
- [ ]
- [ ]
- [ ]
- [ ]
- [ ]

DAIRY / EGGS

- [ ]
- [ ]
- [ ]
- [ ]

GRAINS / BREAD / PASTA

- [ ]
- [ ]
- [ ]
- [ ]
- [ ]

BEVERAGES / SNACKS

- [ ]
- [ ]
- [ ]
- [ ]

NON-FOOD ITEMS

- [ ]
- [ ]
- [ ]

Weekly Meal Planner

15 – 21 RAMADAN

	SUHOOR	IFTAR
15 RAMADAN		
16		
17		
18		
19		
20		
21		

Grocery List

BUDGET:

PRODUCE

- [ ]
- [ ]
- [ ]
- [ ]
- [ ]
- [ ]

MEAT / POULTRY / FISH

- [ ]
- [ ]
- [ ]
- [ ]
- [ ]
- [ ]

DAIRY / EGGS

- [ ]
- [ ]
- [ ]
- [ ]

GRAINS / BREAD / PASTA

- [ ]
- [ ]
- [ ]
- [ ]
- [ ]

BEVERAGES / SNACKS

- [ ]
- [ ]
- [ ]
- [ ]

NON-FOOD ITEMS

- [ ]
- [ ]
- [ ]

Weekly Meal Planner

22 – 28 RAMADAN

	SUHOOR	IFTAR
22 RAMADAN		
23		
24		
25		
26		
27		
28		

Grocery List

BUDGET :

PRODUCE

- [ ]
- [ ]
- [ ]
- [ ]
- [ ]
- [ ]

MEAT / POULTRY / FISH

- [ ]
- [ ]
- [ ]
- [ ]
- [ ]
- [ ]

DAIRY / EGGS

- [ ]
- [ ]
- [ ]
- [ ]

GRAINS / BREAD / PASTA

- [ ]
- [ ]
- [ ]
- [ ]
- [ ]

BEVERAGES / SNACKS

- [ ]
- [ ]
- [ ]
- [ ]

NON-FOOD ITEMS

- [ ]
- [ ]
- [ ]

Weekly Meal Planner

29 – 30 RAMADAN

	SUHOOR	IFTAR
29 RAMADAN		
30		

Notes

_____

_____

_____

_____

_____

_____

_____

Daily
ACTION PLAN
1 – 10 Ramadan

"When Ramadan begins, the gates of
Paradise are opened."

[Sahih Bukhari]

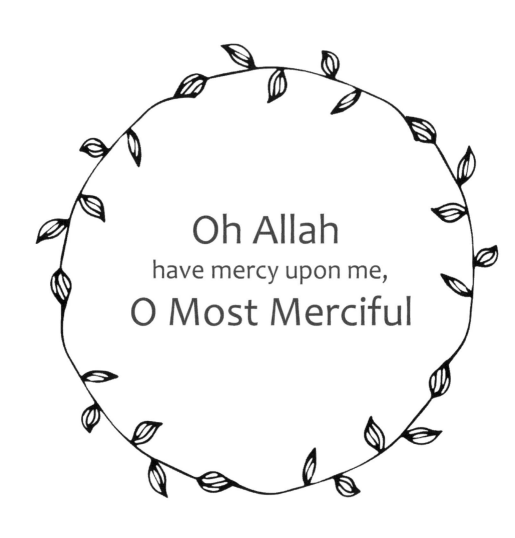

Oh Allah
have mercy upon me,
O Most Merciful

Ramadan Day 1

DATE: _____

TODAY'S GOALS

IBADAH	STATUS	✓
○ FAST		▢
○ SALAH		▢
○ QUR'AN		▢
○ TARAWIH		▢
○ DZIKIR		▢

GOOD DEEDS

		▢
		▢
		▢

ALHAMDULILLAH FOR

Notes

Ramadan Day 2

DATE:

TODAY'S GOALS

IBADAH	STATUS	✓
○ FAST		
○ SALAH		
○ QUR'AN		
○ TARAWIH		
○ DZIKIR		

GOOD DEEDS

ALHAMDULILLAH FOR

Notes

Ramadan Day 3

DATE: _____

TODAY'S GOALS

IBADAH	STATUS	✓
○ FAST		
○ SALAH		
○ QUR'AN		
○ TARAWIH		
○ DZIKIR		

GOOD DEEDS

ALHAMDULILLAH FOR

Notes

Ramadan Day 4

DATE: _____

TODAY'S GOALS

IBADAH	STATUS	✓
◯ FAST		☐
◯ SALAH		☐
◯ QUR'AN		☐
◯ TARAWIH		☐
◯ DZIKIR		☐

GOOD DEEDS

		☐
		☐
		☐

ALHAMDULILLAH FOR

Notes

Ramadan Day 5

DATE: _____

TODAY'S GOALS

IBADAH	STATUS	✓
○ FAST		
○ SALAH		
○ QUR'AN		
○ TARAWIH		
○ DZIKIR		

GOOD DEEDS

ALHAMDULILLAH FOR

Notes

Ramadan Day 6

DATE: _____

TODAY'S GOALS

IBADAH	STATUS	✓
○ FAST		
○ SALAH		
○ QUR'AN		
○ TARAWIH		
○ DZIKIR		

GOOD DEEDS

ALHAMDULILLAH FOR

Notes

Ramadan Day 7

DATE: _____

TODAY'S GOALS

IBADAH	STATUS	✓
○ FAST		
○ SALAH		
○ QUR'AN		
○ TARAWIH		
○ DZIKIR		

GOOD DEEDS

ALHAMDULILLAH FOR

Notes

Ramadan Day 8

DATE: _____

TODAY'S GOALS

IBADAH	STATUS	✓
○ FAST		
○ SALAH		
○ QUR'AN		
○ TARAWIH		
○ DZIKIR		

GOOD DEEDS

ALHAMDULILLAH FOR

Notes

Ramadan Day 9

DATE: _____

TODAY'S GOALS

IBADAH	STATUS	✓
○ FAST		
○ SALAH		
○ QUR'AN		
○ TARAWIH		
○ DZIKIR		

GOOD DEEDS

ALHAMDULILLAH FOR

Notes

Ramadan Day 10

DATE:

TODAY'S GOALS

IBADAH	STATUS	✓
○ FAST		
○ SALAH		
○ QUR'AN		
○ TARAWIH		
○ DZIKIR		

GOOD DEEDS

ALHAMDULILLAH FOR

Notes

Daily
ACTION PLAN
11 – 20 Ramadan

"Indeed there is for the fasting person,
when he breaks his fast, a supplication
which is not rejected".

[Ibn Majah, Al-Hakim]

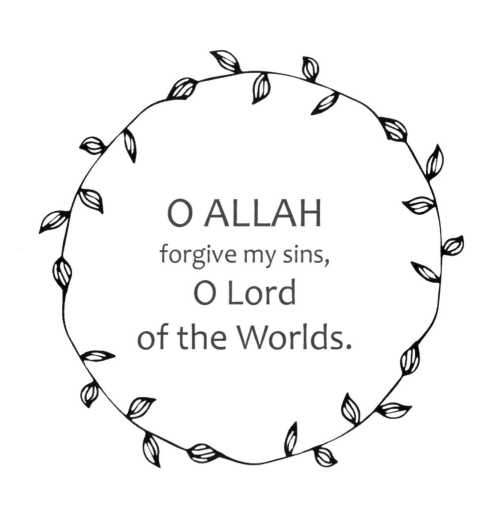

O ALLAH
forgive my sins,
O Lord
of the Worlds.

Ramadan Day 11

DATE:

TODAY'S GOALS

IBADAH	STATUS	✓
◯ FAST		▢
◯ SALAH		▢
◯ QUR'AN		▢
◯ TARAWIH		▢
◯ DZIKIR		▢

GOOD DEEDS

	▢
	▢
	▢

ALHAMDULILLAH FOR

Notes

Ramadan Day 12

DATE: _____

TODAY'S GOALS

IBADAH	STATUS	✓
○ FAST		☐
○ SALAH		☐
○ QUR'AN		☐
○ TARAWIH		☐
○ DZIKIR		☐

GOOD DEEDS

		☐
		☐
		☐

ALHAMDULILLAH FOR

Notes

Ramadan Day 13

DATE: _____

TODAY'S GOALS

IBADAH	STATUS	✓
○ FAST		☐
○ SALAH		☐
○ QUR'AN		☐
○ TARAWIH		☐
○ DZIKIR		☐

GOOD DEEDS

		☐
		☐
		☐

ALHAMDULILLAH FOR

Notes

Ramadan Day 14

DATE: _____

TODAY'S GOALS

IBADAH	STATUS	✓
○ FAST		
○ SALAH		
○ QUR'AN		
○ TARAWIH		
○ DZIKIR		

GOOD DEEDS

ALHAMDULILLAH FOR

Notes

Ramadan Day 15

DATE: _____

TODAY'S GOALS

IBADAH	STATUS	✓
○ FAST		☐
○ SALAH		☐
○ QUR'AN		☐
○ TARAWIH		☐
○ DZIKIR		☐

GOOD DEEDS

		☐
		☐
		☐

ALHAMDULILLAH FOR

Notes

Ramadan Day 16

DATE:

TODAY'S GOALS

IBADAH	STATUS	✓
○ FAST		
○ SALAH		
○ QUR'AN		
○ TARAWIH		
○ DZIKIR		

GOOD DEEDS

ALHAMDULILLAH FOR

Notes

Ramadan Day 17

DATE:

TODAY'S GOALS

IBADAH	STATUS	✓
○ FAST		
○ SALAH		
○ QUR'AN		
○ TARAWIH		
○ DZIKIR		

GOOD DEEDS

ALHAMDULILLAH FOR

Notes

Ramadan Day 18

DATE: _____

TODAY'S GOALS

IBADAH	STATUS	✓
○ FAST		☐
○ SALAH		☐
○ QUR'AN		☐
○ TARAWIH		☐
○ DZIKIR		☐

GOOD DEEDS

		☐
		☐
		☐

ALHAMDULILLAH FOR

Notes

Ramadan Day 19

DATE: _____

TODAY'S GOALS

IBADAH	STATUS	✓
○ FAST		▢
○ SALAH		▢
○ QUR'AN		▢
○ TARAWIH		▢
○ DZIKIR		▢

GOOD DEEDS

		▢
		▢
		▢

ALHAMDULILLAH FOR

Notes

Ramadan Day 20

DATE: _____

TODAY'S GOALS

IBADAH	STATUS	✓
○ FAST		☐
○ SALAH		☐
○ QUR'AN		☐
○ TARAWIH		☐
○ DZIKIR		☐

GOOD DEEDS

☐

☐

☐

ALHAMDULILLAH FOR

Notes

Daily
ACTION PLAN
Last 10 days

"The Night of Power is better than a thousand months."
[Al Qur'an 97 : 3]

"Search for the Night of Qadr in the odd nights of the last ten days of Ramadan."
[Sahih Bukhari]

O ALLAH,
You Alone are
the One who pardons,

and You Alone

love to pardon,
so pardon me.

Ramadan Day 21

DATE: _____

TODAY'S GOALS

IBADAH	STATUS	✓
○ FAST		☐
○ SALAH		☐
○ QUR'AN		☐
○ TARAWIH		☐
○ DZIKIR		☐

GOOD DEEDS

		☐
		☐
		☐

ALHAMDULILLAH FOR

Notes

Ramadan Day 22

DATE: _____

TODAY'S GOALS

IBADAH	STATUS	✓
○ FAST		☐
○ SALAH		☐
○ QUR'AN		☐
○ TARAWIH		☐
○ DZIKIR		☐

GOOD DEEDS

		☐
		☐
		☐

ALHAMDULILLAH FOR

Notes

Ramadan Day 23

DATE: _____

TODAY'S GOALS

IBADAH	STATUS	✓
○ FAST		
○ SALAH		
○ QUR'AN		
○ TARAWIH		
○ DZIKIR		

GOOD DEEDS

ALHAMDULILLAH FOR

Notes

Ramadan Day 24

DATE: _____

TODAY'S GOALS

IBADAH	STATUS	✓
○ FAST		☐
○ SALAH		☐
○ QUR'AN		☐
○ TARAWIH		☐
○ DZIKIR		☐

GOOD DEEDS

	☐
	☐
	☐

ALHAMDULILLAH FOR

Notes

Ramadan Day 25

DATE: _____

TODAY'S GOALS

IBADAH	STATUS	✓
○ FAST		
○ SALAH		
○ QUR'AN		
○ TARAWIH		
○ DZIKIR		

GOOD DEEDS

ALHAMDULILLAH FOR

Notes

Ramadan Day 26

DATE: _____

TODAY'S GOALS

IBADAH	STATUS	✓
○ FAST		☐
○ SALAH		☐
○ QUR'AN		☐
○ TARAWIH		☐
○ DZIKIR		☐

GOOD DEEDS

		☐
		☐
		☐

ALHAMDULILLAH FOR

Notes

Ramadan Day 27

DATE: _____

TODAY'S GOALS

IBADAH	STATUS	✓
○ FAST		▢
○ SALAH		▢
○ QUR'AN		▢
○ TARAWIH		▢
○ DZIKIR		▢

GOOD DEEDS

		▢
		▢
		▢

ALHAMDULILLAH FOR

Notes

Ramadan Day 28

DATE: _____

TODAY'S GOALS

IBADAH	STATUS	✓
○ FAST		☐
○ SALAH		☐
○ QUR'AN		☐
○ TARAWIH		☐
○ DZIKIR		☐

GOOD DEEDS

		☐
		☐
		☐

ALHAMDULILLAH FOR

Notes

Ramadan Day 29

DATE: _____

TODAY'S GOALS

IBADAH	STATUS	✓
○ FAST		▢
○ SALAH		▢
○ QUR'AN		▢
○ TARAWIH		▢
○ DZIKIR		▢

GOOD DEEDS

		▢
		▢
		▢

ALHAMDULILLAH FOR

Notes

Ramadan Day 30

DATE: _____

TODAY'S GOALS

IBADAH	STATUS	✓
○ FAST		▢
○ SALAH		▢
○ QUR'AN		▢
○ TARAWIH		▢
○ DZIKIR		▢

GOOD DEEDS

		▢
		▢
		▢

ALHAMDULILLAH FOR

Notes

TAQABBAL ALLAHU MINNA WA MINKUM

May Allah accept from us, and from you.

Ramadan Reflections

What I have learned this Ramadan ...

Ramadan Reflections

Alhamdulillah, what I have done well ...

_____

_____

_____

_____

_____

_____

_____

_____

_____

_____

_____

_____

_____

_____

_____

_____

_____

Ramadan Reflections

Areas to improve on ...

_____

_____

_____

_____

_____

_____

_____

_____

_____

_____

_____

_____

_____

Ramadan Reflections

In shaa Allah, after this Ramadan
I will continue to ...

_____

_____

_____

_____

_____

_____

_____

_____

_____

_____

_____

"Praise be to ALLAH,
Lord of the Worlds."

[Al Qur'an 1 : 2]

Made in the USA
Middletown, DE
14 March 2023

26768986R00064